Shattered

NATI CARRILLO

Copyright © 2019 Nati Carrillo
All rights reserved
First Edition

PAGE PUBLISHING, INC.
New York, NY

First originally published by Page Publishing, Inc. 2019

ISBN 978-1-64350-384-4 (Paperback)
ISBN 978-1-64350-385-1 (Digital)

Printed in the United States of America

CHAPTER 1

Brittany on Foot

The bell had just rung. Everyone was running toward his or her classes. The halls were becoming quieter as the last doors were slamming shut. The tardy bell had just rung when Brittany arrived on campus. The long walk to school was nothing but short. She had to walk to school Tuesdays and Thursdays because her father, Jake, an insurance agent, worked farther and opposite Brittany's school. Her mother, Clarice, a hairdresser, had to arrive earlier because she had clients waiting by that time. She was a great hairdresser who had all her hair appointments filled a week in advance. The family had only one vehicle, so everyone had to share. However, it was Brittany who had to walk the long way to school, despite rain, heat, or snow. She walked about three miles on those two days. It was enough to frustrate her because she had to leave her home while it was still dark. The other days Brittany got dropped off because Jake didn't have to be in the office, so he worked from home. Jake would drop off his wife,

Clarice, at work, which was thirty miles south from home at seven in the morning. Then rush back to his job twenty miles north and barely make it in time to clock in at eight in the morning. It was a struggle for the entire family, but more for Brittany, who had to walk to school no matter how crazy the weather. She hated it most when she wore nice clothes. She hated to sweat, so she carried an extra set of clothes in her backpack to change if she needed to.

Brittany was sixteen years old, a junior in high school, when puberty struck. It transformed her quite nicely into a beautiful young lady with irresistible curves. She was weighing 125 pounds and had many admirers. Unfortunately, she also had enemies. Enemies whom she thought were her friends. They envied how beautiful she was. The way guys stared at her. It was like if each time they saw her, they were looking at her for the first time. Brittany's friends wanted that same attention. Brittany, however, was so naive she never paid attention to any of her admirers. She wasn't into boys, so she never gave boys a second thought. Brittany had a full set of long blond hair almost reaching her waistline. Her skin was flawless. She had a genuine smile that made everyone smile back at her. Her smile melted even the coldhearted. Her big brown eyes lit when she heard country music. Both her parents loved country music, so it was the music she grew up with. She wanted to sing and dance but didn't feel she was any good at singing or dancing, so she sang and danced in the shower where no one could see or hear her mistakes.

CHAPTER 2

My Circle of Friends

Brittany's friends were of different ages and from different grade levels. Their school enrolled students from sixth to twelfth grades, so not surprisingly, Brittany's friends weren't from her same grade level. Crystal was fourteen years old, a freshman in Brittany's school, and Amanda, her senior friend, was seventeen years old. Sometimes, Brittany would walk with Amanda and Crystal on Tuesdays and Thursdays. Amanda, the oldest, was more of a wild child. She was a venturous and fearless soul. She smoked weed on her way to school with the girls. Crystal was less bold and shy. She was afraid of getting caught, so she dared not walk with Brittany if Amanda was with her. She walked a couple of blocks behind them until Amanda finished her joint. Despite Brittany's religious beliefs, Brittany never confronted Amanda about her smoking. Any and every chance Amanda begged Brittany to try her weed, repeatedly, but Brittany stood her ground replying, "No, I am okay. I don't want to," time and time again. Amanda continued harassing Brittany about not smoking with her but Brittany was just as stubborn. She refused because she knew drugs were dangerous and marijuana was no exception. Brittany never mentioned Amanda's repeated requests to smoke weed to her parents, or else, they would have forbid her from hanging out with Amanda. Brittany needed friends, so she kept it a secret. She figured as long as she wasn't doing the drugs, she was okay.

CHAPTER 3

Amanda's Misfortune

Amanda and Brittany came from two very different support systems. Amanda envied that Brittany had both parents and that they were financially better off. She secretly hated the fact that she was beautiful and had all the guys drooling over her. In Amanda's eyes, Brittany had the life and was the person Amanda wished she could be. Amanda didn't care to share her true feelings with Brittany. All Amanda cared about was gaining Brittany's trust to set her up for failure. She hated her that much. Unfortunately, Brittany was a young and naive girl that couldn't tell her real friends from her worst enemies.

Amanda's parents were divorced. The two divorced just shortly after Amanda was born; so, Julia, Amanda's mother, blamed her for Carl, leaving them. Carl, Amanda's father had issues of his own and was wanted by the law. Carl enjoyed his sleep before Amanda was born and couldn't stand her constant crying. It was just too much for him that he abandoned both of them without saying goodbye. It had only been two weeks after Amanda's birth that Carl decided to leave the house. Julia fell into a deep depression one month after Amanda's birth. Julia started drinking. Julia drank every day all day. She soon forgot about Amanda. Julia left Amanda with random people her so-called girl or boyfriends for days at a time. Those so-called friends didn't care to feed, bathe her, or nourish her as she or any child deserved. They treated her like a housekeeper. At the very young age of five, Amanda was washing dishes, cleaning toilets and mopping floors. She was requested often to mop the floor for those that didn't know how to hold their liquor. If Amanda didn't clean correctly, she would be spanked and forced to kneel in a corner for hours.

Amanda's body wasn't physically mature to clean as an adult could; so, as a result, she was punished repeatedly. Her caretakers made her spend most of her young life off to a corner on her knees. By the age of five, Amanda had learned to hate the world. She hated her mother, her father, and the strangers that abused her. Amanda couldn't trust anyone and resented her mother for giving her such a horrible life.

Amanda had no role models. She knew no one cared for her. It's like she never existed to anyone except older men who took advantage of her repeatedly. Julia was always drunk that she never noticed when her boyfriends abused her little girl. As a result, Amanda developed a post-traumatic stress disorder.

SHATTERED

She wasn't able to sleep. The fear of men coming into her room was emotionally disturbing. If Amanda slept for two hours, it was enough—to call it, a good night's rest for her.

CHAPTER 4

Monsters in My Bed

Amanda knew the night was going to be long and horrid. The door screeched as it opened slowly. She saw a tall dark figure walking toward her. He was holding a beer in one hand and a cigar in the other. He stepped closer, tippy-toeing closer toward her. As he was putting his beer down, Amanda tried to run. She sprung out of bed, but he quickly grabbed her and pulled her onto the bed. Amanda was kicking and screaming all the while, but the man quickly tied his belt around her mouth to stop her from shouting for help. While holding her down, he used his large rugged hands to hold hers and used his knees to press her legs to prevent her from kicking.

"He is very heavy. Too heavy to push off. The more I struggle, the more he beats me. He threatens to make my life worse and slaps me. By this time, my face is burning. He is too heavy for me to fight him. My legs are tingly and burning. Please, someone help me!"

SHATTERED

He screamed at her to touch him. "Grab me. You will like it. I promise!"

The more Amanda refused to do as he requested, the worse he shoved and squeezed his fingers underneath her underwear. He grabbed her tiny hands and pulled them toward his crotch. He proceeded to unzip his pants. She tried with all her might to kick him off, but to no avail, she failed. He ripped her dress open and removed her panties. Fearing the worst, she turned away and tightly closed her eyes. She didn't want to see him or any of it. He forcibly turned her face toward him and started kissing her face while rubbing his penis against her. All of a sudden, she opened her eyes wider than ever as she felt an awful thrust into her small body. The tearing of flesh, a gush of warm contents, and a dreadful burning pain was all Amanda felt. She tried to yell and cry, but no one heard. No one came to save her from this horrible monster that stole her innocence.

The ordeal lasted way too long; it was way too much trauma for her little body to handle. The pain was just too much that she prayed for it to be over, and she didn't even believe in God. Finally, a final moan, a heavy sigh, and he lay motionless on top of her. Just like that, it all stopped. He continued to kiss her chest and face and let her know he cared for her.

"It's all for love, sweetie."

As he untied the belt and started removing it from her mouth, he threatened to do it again if she told anyone or yelled for help. She dared not make a sound. He got up, zipped his pants, grabbed his beer, lit his cigarette, and left the room. Amanda was left bleeding, crying, and barely able to walk. She tried to stand but was not able to walk, so she dragged herself into the bathroom where she put herself in the shower for hours. Amanda desperately tried to eradicate the scent that monster had left all over her. She washed her face, arms, and legs for such a long time that she caused herself more bleeding. Not being able to scrub between her legs, Amanda ran the hot water over her private areas in efforts to remove all his bodily fluids. It was steaming hot that the bathroom started looking like a sauna. Amanda didn't react until she noticed blisters showing up over her pelvic and abdominal regions. She finally turned off the water and just lay there, motionless, imagining she was anywhere else but there. She didn't move; she couldn't—her pain was intolerable. No one missed her, and it was clear that no one cared. That night was only the beginning of her living nightmare.

From that day on, she hated everything that was beautiful and everyone who laughed around her. Julia didn't find out about the incident with that horrible monster or any other stranger that abused Amanda. She was too drunk and always passed out. She saw nothing, heard nothing, and did nothing. Amanda meant nothing to Julia; it was obvious. Amanda lay in bed for days, and Julia never noticed she was out of sight. The only person she was not invisible to was that monster. He kept coming back to Amanda's room almost every night. He started to take her food. She learned to obey and do as he wished. She no longer resisted or fought him because he was much nicer to her when she did what he wanted.

The ugly sweat dripping off his chest, the large callused hands groping her little body, and the smell of alcohol infiltrated Amanda so profoundly she started to miss him when he didn't show up. She began to believe in her confused mind that he cared for her. In fact, she genuinely thought he was the only one who cared for her at all. Even if it was to have her, his need to have her, was enough for Amanda to believe she was not invisible to the world.

CHAPTER 5

My World Shattered

No one heard her plea for help that night or any night after that one. No one cared that this ugly monster kept stealing her dreams or that he took her life and robbed her of her innocence. It was there that Amanda started to hate the world around her and vowed to hate everyone. She never understood what happened to her that night, but she didn't have anyone to tell. There was no one to comfort her, to hold her, or tell Amanda everything would be okay. She was alone in a cruel world.

His horrid scent and heavy hands covering her tiny face almost suffocating her were unbearable. She made believe she was in a happy world every time he returned to have her. The opening of that squeaky door produced so much anxiety that Amanda started to leave the door open. Of course, that horrible monster thought she was expecting him and grew proud of his actions. Pretty soon, he walked in with much more confidence; in his sick mind, he truly believed she cared for him. Both were confused in their own worlds. He started to wear strong smelling colognes, combed his shaggy gray hair, and trotted himself to her room as if he was going to meet his girl. He was growing so confident that he started to leave the door open as he left; yet still, no one noticed that horrible monster in her room. He was the only one who saw her. He was the only connection to human touch that Amanda ever experienced growing up, and even though it was a forbidden and evil encounter, she learned to accept him. He had a wife and kids, but that didn't stop him from committing his gruesome crime over and over. Her monster had no guilt, no heart, no remorse. He was a sick man.

Amanda started picking up coins and stealing money from the drunken people she cleaned after day after day. They never found out Amanda was taking their money because they were drunk and experienced blackouts. Amanda was safe they would never find out what or how much money she had taken. As soon as Amanda was able to gather enough money she thought was needed, she ran away from that home. She found a place at a nearby park where she would sleep on benches for days. Amanda's money ran out soon after she left. When she got hungry, Amanda had to beg and dig into trashcans for food. A few weeks later, she was informed that homeless shelters could house her. She searched for them and as soon as she found one, she stayed there. She was doing well, up until, the shelter advised her she had to move on because she had reached the maximum length of stay, which was two months. She was deeply upset, *Who runs you off or tells you to leave a homeless shelter? There is no good in this world. Everyone is evil, What a disgrace!*

Amanda hated her life.

CHAPTER 6

Crystal

Crystal was just fourteen years old. A freshman in the same high school as Amanda and Brittany. Her parents were Simon and Ruth. Simon worked as a farm worker, and Ruth was a stay-home mom. Crystal had two older brothers, Thomas and Dillon. They were an average family earning an average salary. They had family problems, but the parents managed to stay and keep it together. They were strict parents with Crystal because she was the youngest and the only girl in the family. Crystal's brothers were overprotective of their little sister and heard every phone conversation she had. Crystal hated it, but she didn't mind it after a while. She would ignore them. She was warned by her brothers not to hang around with Amanda or Brittany because they were much older and more experienced. Thomas knew Amanda's past and dreaded his little sister having an association with someone who had a troubled past. He warned her repeatedly, but Crystal did her own thing; she was a teenager. She didn't care as long as she didn't get influenced to smoke by her. She knew to stay away as soon as Amanda lit that joint.

CHAPTER 7

Lusting Brittany

Amanda's friends were mostly guy friends in twelfth grade or had already graduated. They asked Amanda for Brittany's phone number and address, but Amanda insisted she wasn't their type and refused to reveal that information. Amanda knew Brittany's daily routine. Brittany trusted her. When Amanda grew desperate, she would reveal Brittany's whereabouts to her boyfriends in exchange for her weed. Brittany didn't care or notice that guys were always around her; it was no accident. She was a smart, beautiful, and curvy young lady with a great personality. Amanda hated that Brittany was *that* desired and loved by everyone.

Amanda skipped classes often to smoke. She loved to hang around older guys. Amanda hated having sex, but when she had it, she would have sex with older men who shared their weed and beer with her. She had this one guy she preferred to be around. His name was Lucas. He was thirty years old. They were together for about three years up until Lucas started paying more attention to Brittany. He preferred being around Brittany all the time. Brittany didn't pay attention, and she thought Lucas was just friendly. She knew he was Amanda's boyfriend. Besides, he was too old, and she was not a bit interested in guys yet. Lucas had several friends who lusted Brittany also. They were pretty much competing with each other to see which one would get her attention. Brittany didn't pay any attention to anyone. Soon after, they started making negative comments about her. They started degrading Brittany as she walked by them and commented, "Look this way, honey. We are your real men!" Brittany never turned to face them, which made them angry. Brittany had one thing on her mind, school, and nothing else. She was smart but very immature about guys. Men or boys were the last things on her mind.

Lucas, Mark, and Paul hated that day after day she carelessly walked beside them without acknowledging their male presence. They whispered and whistled as Brittany and Amanda walked by and said things like, "Sweetie, look, we have what you need!"

Brittany ignored them. She was preoccupied with her school projects and speaking to Amanda. Amanda knew damn well what was going on but brushed it off. Crystal noticed how those old men drooled over Brittany every time. She lagged behind and was disgusted by their behavior. Brittany, however, never gave those men the time of day, which infuriated them even more. Those unimportant and insecure men grew so obsessed with Brittany's inattentions; they developed a plan to meet with her.

CHAPTER 8

From Boyfriend to Friend

Amanda, on the other hand, was furious because Lucas was not paying attention to her anymore, so she wasn't able to get weed from him. She had to revert to Mark, and Mark was also getting infatuated with Brittany. Amanda tried to call Lucas, but he didn't answer his phone. Running out of weed made her desperate because she was starting to remember her horrible past. She stopped by his house, and even though he wasn't home, Amanda did not leave empty-handed.

As she approached Lucas's home, she noticed his car wasn't in the driveway, so she started walking away. Suddenly, she heard a man call out, "Can I help you? Are you looking for Lucas?"

Amanda quickly turned back and noticed a much older man standing by the door. He was tall, dark, with broad shoulders, and a long white beard. As she walked toward him, he stared at her strangely. He looked at her from top to bottom, licking his lower lip while touching his crotch. He stretched his hand to greet her.

"Hi, I am Brutus. I am staying with Lucas for a short time. I am a traveler, just passing by. Who might this pretty lady be?"

Amanda's face flushed as she replied, "I am Amanda, Lucas's friend. I just wanted to ask Lucas for a joint, but seeing that he is not here, I will leave and come back at a later time. Sorry to bother you, sir."

"Why the rush, little lady? I have a shit load of weed. Want to come in?"

Amanda knew it was wrong, but she felt neglected because Lucas was not paying attention to her anymore. She needed weed, so she went inside.

As he started to roll a joint, he asked her what he was getting in return. Amanda began to remove her clothes and sat on his lap.

He chuckled and said, "Well, aren't you a naughty girl?"

Brutus was distracted and stopped rolling the joint and quickly grabbed and kissed Amanda's breasts. Amanda finished rolling the joint; she lit it and started smoking. She was so relieved to have a joint that she didn't even notice Brutus coming. It had been three whole days since her last smoke. She was glad she stopped by Lucas's place. She got what she needed and somewhat enjoyed this man's company. She couldn't understand why this older man made her feel good, safe, and at peace even if it was for a short while. He was quick with his business, so she got up and dressed. Brutus was somewhat confused because she had no expression of pleasure or disgust after their encounter. No discussions, no regrets, and no future plans were discussed. Brutus stared at Amanda and couldn't help wonder what was going on in her little head besides the urge to smoke; he knew she was unhappy and emotionally unstable. Brutus didn't say or ask her anything. Amanda didn't either, she just left. Brutus knew she was Lucas's girl, but she didn't care so he didn't ask. She was willing, he was ready, and a man never turns down an opportunity to get laid.

CHAPTER 9

Her Last Walk

It was Tuesday, six thirty in the morning, one of the many days Brittany had to walk to school. Crystal was sick at home with a cold, so she wasn't with Amanda and Brittany that day. It was still dark and barely visible, as the girls walked down the road to school. Amanda informed Brittany she learned of a new and shorter way to school, which would help them save time and arrive earlier. Amanda begged Brittany to use the new shortcut. Brittany hesitated to use the shortcut at first, but finally agreed, so they did. Brittany was uneasy about this new route, but she trusted Amanda. They headed deep into the dark woods. Both of them carried backpacks. Brittany carried her books, an extra set of clothes, and shoes as usual but Amanda carried her stash of weed.

They had walked for about five minutes into the woods when all of a sudden the sound of breaking branches brought them to a halt.

SHATTERED

As Brittany turned, Amanda yelled at Brittany, "Watch out!" Before Brittany could see who was running toward her, she felt a strong pull. Someone grabbed her from behind, covered her head with a cloth, and then smashed her with an object.

Brittany instantly felt a gush of warm fluid over her head. Then through her eyelids, there was some red—a significant amount of bright red blood was flowing down her forehead. She had been hit with a large heavy metal. Suddenly, Brittany's legs weakened. She lost her balance and then fell to the ground. She tried calling out to Amanda, but she couldn't scream because there was a hairy and heavy hand jabbing into her mouth while another person was ripping and pulling off her shirt and pants. Suddenly, Amanda's yelling stopped.

Brittany heard several male voices laughing and breaking bottles but couldn't see who they were. The brown cloth had tiny holes, but there wasn't enough daylight to see because her eyes were full of blood. She felt more than two hands touching her body. It was awful. When they finally removed the cloth from her face, it was only to enjoy her thoroughly. They wanted to see her beauty while they stole her innocence and had her repeatedly. They were wearing black masks of some sort so she couldn't see who they were. She couldn't help thinking she had heard their voices before.

There were four men; they seemed much older than the guys in her school because of their deep voices. Their hands were much hairier, more robust, and calloused as they groped her. These men were not from her school. She knew that much. Both her hands had been tied with a very prickly rope. It was very tight, so tight that with every attempt to free from it, it cut deeper into her wrists. She couldn't help wonder who and why they would want to harm them. All through that terrible ordeal, she kept wondering what happened to Amanda.

Brittany kept kicking and screaming but was unable to make a sound through the sweaty hand pressing over her mouth. She could taste her blood, and soon after she had to swallow it, or she would drown in it. She was losing so much blood. She wondered why no one heard them or saw them. *Surely someone had to walk by*, she thought. Then she remembered, they had wandered off the main road. It was then she knew no one would find or help them. For the first time during that dreadful and painful ordeal, Brittany started crying.

CHAPTER 10

Sweet Revenge

Tears poured down her face. She was helpless as she had to endure that horrible act of humiliation. They took turns with her. They laughed and mocked her as they had their way with her. It was just too painful to endure. The first one had a tattoo of a demon on his chest and reeked of cinnamon liquor. He ripped her panty off, fondled her, then jammed his finger inside her. After he got tired of doing that, he thrust himself into her forcefully. He was so rough Brittany felt a sheering, burning, and ripping pain as he raped her. She tried to scream, but nothing came out. She felt a burn, a tear, and then a warm gush of something down her legs.

He kept saying, "Now you know, bitch. You wouldn't give me the time or day. Now I take it all from you. You will remember me, arrogant bitch, for the rest of your life!"

As he got off, another man got on top. She prayed for all of it to be over, but it wouldn't end.

The second man was even stronger, heavier, and much meaner than the first. He couldn't bear for her to see him while he was coming. He covered her eyes and thrust himself into her. Her pain worsened with each thrust. As he was raping her, the other was holding her head down. The one positioned by her head unzipped his pants, took out his erect penis, and started rubbing himself on her face. It was clear these men were sick. They were enjoying each other while the other performed their unimaginable deed.

The third guy flipped Brittany over, fondled her with his fingers, then penetrated her. Just as she thought, it couldn't get any worse; she felt a painful tear. There was a lot of burning as he repeatedly thrust himself forcefully into her. She prayed for it to stop; it was far too much.

The last guy intentionally broke a beer bottle smirking and laughing as he flipped Brittany over. He then whispered offensive words into her ear, "Such a beauty. Now why would God make such a beautiful creature that men can't enjoy? Well, I am enjoying her now!"

He turned her back facing down then thrust his erect penis into her. The man grew insanely furious when he couldn't enjoy Brittany anymore. There was so much blood and body fluids that his penis slipped right out. Three men had already had her, so it was far too wet and bloody. Even though it was very bloody, that didn't stop this man from having his way with her.

SHATTERED

He whispered into Brittany's ear, "Well, if I can't enjoy you this way, I will make damn sure every man knows I was here." He again whispered into her ear, "I will make you prettier and more desirable to every man."

He took the broken bottle, started smashing it into her vaginal area while biting on her breasts, biting off some breast tissue then proceeded to ejaculate onto her face. She screamed in pain, but by this time, her voice was gone, not a sound came out. She wanted to kick, to make him stop, but she could no longer move. It was then she surrendered. She stopped fighting for she was too weak. Brittany wished herself dead at that very moment. While getting raped, she looked over and noticed Amanda lying there, lifeless.

The other three men were throwing and breaking bottles at Amanda as if they were signing her body and enjoying their sick behavior. Amanda wasn't moving anymore, and Brittany couldn't run. She remained helpless. Suddenly, Brittany felt a glimpse of hope when their voices sounded as if they were walking away. Then nothing—no more breaking of bottles and no more laughter was heard. By this time, it was daylight, but Brittany was in complete darkness. It was at that very instant, Brittany was ready to give up. Finally, she felt peace. Brittany wanted to yell at Amanda and let her know she was alive but she was too weak, almost lifeless.

Suddenly, Brittany became cold and started shivering. She couldn't open her eyes anymore and saw complete darkness. She was okay with it because she finally had and felt peace. Death would be sweeter than the pain she was experiencing at that very moment. She was ready to die if it was her time. The last thing Brittany remembered before falling unconscious was the sound of sirens. Brittany and Amanda were found bruised, bleeding, and grossly disfigured. Both girls were still alive and barely hanging on to dear life. Once in the ambulance, one paramedic was starting intravenous lines and preventing further blood loss while the other was trying to find family phone numbers to inform them of the hospital they were taking them.

By the time the ambulance arrived at the hospital; Jake and Clarice were already waiting at the emergency room. Jake and Clarice were worried and demanded information on their daughter's condition. Amanda's mom, Julia, was nowhere around. All efforts were being made to contact Julia because hospital policy required it of all minors. Amanda was one month from her eighteenth birthday. They sent out the local police to find Julia because they still needed family. The first stretcher went by leaving a trail of bright blood everywhere. It was Brittany.

Jake shouted at his daughter hoping she could hear him, "Brittany, it's daddy. I am here baby girl!"

She heard her mother crying uncontrollably telling her to fight for her life, to wake up, and not to give up. Brittany managed to open her swollen eyes for a split second; just enough to see her parents, then fell into a deep sleep.

SHATTERED

As they were moving Brittany from the stretcher to the bed in the emergency room, her heart stopped. She flatlined and stopped breathing. The nurses pushed a button on the wall, then all the nurses and doctors ran to Brittany's side. They called a code blue. Jake and Clarice were asked to step away and let the nurses and doctors work on their daughter. Since her clothes had been ripped off, it was easier to apply the electrodes after wiping some blood off her chest. They shocked Brittany twice; it was awful. Her body jolted with each shock, but finally after the second shock, there was a heartbeat. Clarice was in complete denial and refused to accept what had been done to her little girl.

Brittany looked fragile. Some skin on her cheeks was missing. Her eyes swollen shut, her arms, and legs extensively bruised and bleeding, and you couldn't tell if what you were staring at was muscle, tendon, or bone that was exposed. Blood everywhere—from the cuts in her face, neck, arms, chest, inner and outer thighs, and legs, the sight was horrific. There was so much blood loss.

Jake was in disbelief mumbling, "My baby girl, what have they done to her?" and started sobbing uncontrollably. Nurses were hanging bags of intravenous fluids (IV) back to back and requesting consent for blood transfusions. She lost more than half her blood. Jake and Clarice both agreed to try everything possible to bring her back. She received multiple blood transfusions and IV fluid, but Brittany was still pale and lifeless. They finally inserted a breathing tube because Brittany had been through so much. She had lost so much blood that her heart wasn't pumping fast enough and her brain was not getting sufficient oxygen. All her organs were shutting down so she was not able to breathe on her own anymore. It was a horrific sight for anyone to see. Jake and Clarice started praying. They prayed and hoped that their daughter would pull through this horrible ordeal.

CHAPTER 11

Questioning Faith

Once their daughter was intubated, they moved her to the MICCU or medical intensive critical care unit where Brittany spent the next several weeks in a coma and on life support. Her face was so severely disfigured from the broken bottles that nurses had to wrap gauze bandages to prevent infection reaching to her exposed skin. The dressings kept saturating through with blood and in order to keep them dry and free from infection, the nurses had to change them several times a day. Eventually, Brittany would require skin grafts to her face, arms, chest, thighs, and legs, but all medical priorities were directed on stabilizing Brittany's medical condition first. Meanwhile, Brittany's friend, Amanda had already coded twice, and doctors feared the worst for her. Her mother, Julia, was still nowhere to be found. They had to leave Amanda on a breathing tube because she had lost a lot of blood. Even though she was stabilized for a while, her condition was getting worse. She acquired an infection from having multiple surgeries and not responding well to antibiotics. She was also transferred to the MICCU unit and doctors waited for Julia.

Clarice slept in the waiting area most nights because they didn't allow her to sleep in Brittany's room. She left work early to be with her daughter, hoping she would wake up. The moment visiting hours began, Clarice anxiously stayed at Brittany's bedside. Clarice would read and have Brittany listen to country music for hours. Jake kneeled by his daughter's bed every morning and prayed for her recovery. He begged, cried, and wished she would show a sign that she heard him.

Despite the long hours and sacrifices they made for their daughter, their prayers, music, and faith worked. Brittany was responding well to the medications and treatment. Clarice, on the other hand, was growing anxious and frustrated that she began lashing out at God. "*Where were you when this was happening to my daughter. How could you let this happen?*"

It was then that Jake walked in. "Honey," Jake replied, "God is right here keeping her alive. She is holding on. She hasn't let go."

She got up, wanting, and wishing to punch Jake for not understanding her pain, but instead, cried uncontrollably. Jake hugged her then Clarice shouted, "How could anyone do this to our baby girl? How? Look at her. She was so perfect, beautiful, and now that beauty was taken from her. They left her face disfigured. She will have those terrible scars forever. A constant reminder of that day for the rest of her life!"

Jake tried to comfort his wife as best he could but still, they both cried.

Suddenly, Clarice felt a slight tug at her dress behind her. It was Brittany. She was trying to grab her mother to talk. Jake noticed Brittany was trying to speak. Her face was still bandaged so they couldn't see her expressions. "Look, honey, she is waking up!"

Laughing and crying all at once. They both got closer to see their daughter's eyes for the first time in weeks. Jake was smiling with Brittany as she held his hand too. Tears filled her eyes, but she couldn't talk with the tube in her mouth. She signaled for a pen and paper to write. Both parents were smiling and crying.

They gave her a notepad, and the first words she wrote read, "I love you, Mom and Dad. I am so sorry!"

"Sorry?" her mother cried out. "Why on earth would you be sorry, baby? Why? You have nothing to be sorry about."

Brittany wrote again with tears. "You were worried about me."

Her mother dropped the notepad and quickly hugged Brittany. "I am so glad you're back baby, so glad. Thank you, Jesus!"

All the nurses were cheering around and crying excitedly. It was an awesome sight. Jake couldn't hold back and started kissing his daughter's forehead stating, "We missed you, baby girl. We love you so much!"

That same day, Alan, the investigator heard Brittany had awakened so he stopped by Brittany's room to speak with her. Brittany couldn't communicate well; so, she wrote one line to the investigator. "Come back tomorrow. I want to cherish this moment a bit longer!"

Alan nodded and left the room respecting her wishes. Later that day, the doctor removed the tube. Brittany was breathing on her own. She was able to speak but in low voice because the breathing tube had caused some trauma to her vocal cords. Her voice was hoarse. She was able to take ice chips. Doctors wanted to make sure she was able to swallow without difficulties before feeding her. It had been several hours when she realized she had to face the fact that something horrible happened to her; nasty men had taken her virtue.

She didn't want to recall the experience, but she knew she had to speak of it to the investigator. Those men needed to be caught. She got angry. Brittany cried the whole day. She questioned her faith. "Why me? Why us?"

At that moment, she realized she hadn't asked about Amanda, so she called the nurses to ask about Amanda's condition. She wanted to know if she was okay. They advised Brittany that Amanda was still in a coma and fighting for her life. Brittany was relieved that Amanda was still alive.

CHAPTER 12

Unrecognizable

While in the MICCU, no one visited Amanda. The nurses spoke to Amanda on and off, but it wasn't the same. She had no family support, no love, no nurturing, no reason to live, and no one to live for. Amanda's prognosis was grim. She wasn't responding well to treatments. Her facial skin grafts weren't healing as expected, and her blood infection wasn't responding well to any of the antibiotics they had tried. Her legs were severely swollen and so disfigured from the trauma that doctors feared she would need an amputation of both limbs. Amanda wasn't looking well, and Julia hadn't been located yet. Doctors required consents, so they tried to reach Amanda's father, Carl, but he had fled the country. Carl was a fugitive. So while her legs rotted (grew gangrenous), and her life escaped her every breath (dying), Amanda was left alone. Alone again and in pain, or maybe she had no pain, but the sad truth was that no one was available to take her home, speak with her, stimulate, or motivate her to live. She probably had no need to live.

The nurses hadn't seen such a sad case before. They needed reassurance and spiritual healing. It was difficult to see her fade away day after day. She had been through so much it was difficult to imagine she would ever want to come back. She had to have her breasts reconstructed due to deep lacerations caused by the broken bottles. She had to have her mutilated uterus, ovaries, and fallopian tubes removed due to severe trauma caused by insertion of broken bottles into her vagina and rectal walls. They had to close her rectum because it was severed and scarred. Her rectum could not serve the purpose of defecating anymore. The doctors were forced to place a colostomy and urostomy bag. Every organ in Amanda's body was harmed in some way or form. It was unbelievable how much destruction those men caused her. What a life it would be for her if she woke up. She would have to learn how to manage all her drains. It wasn't a dream she was going to wake up from; it was going to be a harsh reality. Her life was no longer going to be the same when and if she woke up.

Three weeks had passed after the rape when Amanda's breathing tube was removed. Everyone thought for sure she was going to stop breathing, but Amanda continued breathing on her own. She was still holding on for what or whom, no one knew. There was no one there for her. Her entire life had been a struggle; yet, for some reason, she wasn't ready to go.

CHAPTER 13

The Perpetrators

The cops were able to identify the men who raped the girls because they didn't use condoms. There was actual DNA (deoxyribonucleaic acid) recovered from the scene and on the girls. It would be an easy case to solve. The men didn't seem to care; it's like they wanted to be discovered. These men had every ill intention of hurting those girls, and they did. Those men were still on the run. The DNA found on Brittany's fluids matched those of Lucas, Jimmy, Mark and Paul. In Amanda's rape, the evidence implicated Lucas, Mark, Paul, and Brutus. However, Amanda had been with Brutus before so they didn't know whether he was involved in plotting the rape. Still, there was an arrest warrant for him until he could prove otherwise.

Lucas was quite bothered when his neighbor told him that his girl had had an encounter with Brutus the day before. Amanda had been Lucas's girlfriend for years, so it was obvious he had a valid motive to go after Amanda. He was enraged at her, so he was suspect number one. It was the perfect plan for revenge. Lucas knew Amanda hated Brittany because she was the one who told them she was going to lure her into the woods, away from the road so that they could have their way with her. She never anticipated anything happening to her. Betrayal, jealousy, and envy all surrounded this case.

Lucas's plan never included hurting or raping Amanda, but Lucas let the men have their way with Amanda because to him, she was a whore. Her plan to harm Brittany backfired. The men were justifying their actions because she betrayed Lucas. The whole rape was an act of rage and revenge. Lucas couldn't comprehend why Amanda would easily betray their relationship. She so willingly gave herself to Brutus without any shame or remorse. Her act of promiscuity made him snap.

CHAPTER 14

Poor Excuse for a Mother

In a desperate attempt to locate Julia, the hospital made a public statement offering monetary compensation to anyone with information leading to Julia's whereabouts. Ironically, the same day, the media aired such statement, Julia herself showed up at the hospital. Julia didn't hesitate and asked, "Do I get the money if I showed up on my own account?" The nurses were appalled. This woman didn't even ask about her daughter's condition. Amanda was dying, the nurses thought, *what a poor excuse for a mother*. The doctor was paged because he needed to speak to Julia.

"Ma'am, are you Julia, Amanda's mother?"

"Who?" She must have been stoned or on something because she was not answering questions adequately.

"Are you Amanda's mother?"

"Well, that depends on who is asking and what she has done."

The doctor grew furious. "Ma'am, your daughter was repeatedly raped and disfigured and is currently in a coma. As we speak, she may even be dying!"

Julia looked up at the doctor and laughed. "Well, she got what she deserved. She stole my life, my men, and she was responsible for Carl leaving me. As a baby, she wouldn't stop crying. Her father didn't love her either. Poor girl."

The doctor didn't want to cause a scene, so he walked off. Mumbling to the nurses as he walked off, "Good luck with that one!"

The nurses couldn't believe this woman's attitude. They didn't want to show her to Amanda's room anymore.

Julia asked, "Well, where is the brat?"

The nurses notified child protective services hoping to arrest her but that didn't happen. The nurse walked with Julia to Amanda's room. As soon as she walked into the room, Julia walked to the window and mumbled, "It's a pity you can't see this beautiful view."

The nurse angrily stared at Julia. As Julia walked to Amanda, she looked over to the nurse and asked if she could still hear.

The nurse attempted to remove Julia from the room, but Julia pulled away. "Wait, you called me. Why do you want to get rid of me so soon? I need to see her die!"

"Well, if you have nothing good to say, don't say anything at all. Amanda can hear, but you know that, right!"

"Yeah, well let her hear me. She got what she deserved. She was the cause of my dear Carl leaving us. She stole my men and she made my life an absolute nightmare. So yeah, she should hear that!"

The nurse called security to have her removed from Amanda's room at once. The nurse was pulling on Julia taking her toward the door.

As she was leaving the room, she yelled back to Amanda, "Just leave, Amanda, your life is nothing, and no one will love you like that!"

The nurse started crying and begged Julia, "Shut up. Just please, shut up! Please leave!"

It had been just an hour after Julia left when Amanda's heart stopped. She finally gave up. She had been holding on to dear life expecting her mother's forgiveness and love, but when that didn't happen, Amanda stopped breathing. She passed away. It was clear Julia hated her daughter.

Soon after Amanda passed, they called Julia, but the only words she muttered were, "Well, I'll be damned, she heard me," *laughing*.

She didn't go back to claim the body or do any preparations for Amanda's funeral. She claimed she had no money to bury her, so she never returned to the hospital. That was the saddest case and situation the hospital staff had ever experienced in their entire nursing life. The nurses and doctors cried for weeks following Amanda's death.

CHAPTER 15

The Untold Confession

The next day, Brittany knew what she had to do, so she prepared herself emotionally for the dreadful interview with the investigator. The investigator, Alan, arrived at the hospital, sat next to Brittany, and started recording the events of that Tuesday morning. Brittany stopped halfway through the interview. She froze and stared at the wall. Alan tried to bring her back, but it was useless.

"Brittany, can you hear me?"

She couldn't speak. Her mouth began to tremble. Her hands began to shake, and tears ran down her cheeks. Her heart monitor and blood pressure machine started going off. Pretty soon, the nurses were in her room. Alan moved out of the way, as the nurses started to check Brittany. Her heart rate was two hundred-twenty, and her blood pressure increased to 160 over 90. They insisted he leave the room. Clearly, Brittany was not ready or able to handle any questioning yet. It was too soon.

Brittany got so worked up during the interview that doctors had to induce a coma. They were worried she would have a stroke; her blood pressure was dangerously elevated. While in a medically induced coma, Brittany had vivid dreams of the incident. Her blood pressure was not responding to the blood pressure medications. Her blood pressure was up to 200/110, and heart rate was steady at 144 with respirations of 34. It seemed she was fighting. Her body was shaking constantly. It was obvious; she was reliving that horrible day; the doctors had to physically restrain her and keep her heavily sedated. No one knew what to do, only hope and pray that the medications she was given would soon work to decrease her blood pressure. Brittany's chances of leaving the hospital alive were not favorable anymore. Her emotional status was fragile, and her physical state was already severely compromised.

CHAPTER 16

The Nightmare Continues

Doctors gradually pulled Brittany out of her induced coma. She was doing well when all of a sudden, Brittany started developing nausea with vomiting. She received anti-nausea medication that made her drowsy all day, but soon after the medication wore off, she woke up with extreme hunger. She asked her mother to bring her some homemade soup because she couldn't stand the sight of hospital food anymore. So Clarice did as her baby girl asked. When Clarice showed up with the soup, the minute Brittany uncovered the dish, she started gagging, wanting to throw up.

She grew upset and questioned, "How can I feel so hungry, crave certain foods, and not be able to eat them? Why, this is so frustrating?" Both parents and two nurses were in the room when Brittany questioned her behavior. At that moment, they all looked at each other. There was a long pause; some distressing looks were exchanged then Jake ran outside.

"What? What happened? Why did Dad leave? Was he upset? What did I do wrong?"

Clarice rushed to Brittany, hugged her, and reassured her she had done nothing wrong. "Baby, you did nothing wrong. Dad just remembered he had to call his boss and let him know he was not going back to work today. That's all, nothing else."

Brittany naively asked again, "Well, what is the matter with me? Why am I hungry yet can't tolerate any food?"

Clarice asked Brittany to wait while she checked up on Jake. Once outside, Clarice headed to the nurse's station to ask, "Is there a possibility that my daughter could be pregnant?" she asked, sobbing.

The nurse anxiously responded, "I will call her doctor, explain her symptoms, and let you know what he orders."

The nurse reassured Clarice, not to worry until the urine and blood results came back. "However, if any one of the men didn't use condoms, which was my understanding from the police report, there is a great possibility she might be. I am sorry."

Clarice couldn't bear the thought of her little girl being raped, tortured, mutilated, and left to die by these callous monsters then leave their seed behind to torment her for the rest of her life. It was just too much. Clarice had to be taken to the emergency room because she felt she was having a heart attack. She requested the nurses not tell Brittany which lab tests she was going to have drawn, just in case her daughter was pregnant. Clarice wanted to be the one to break the news to Brittany if in fact she were pregnant.

CHAPTER 17

Panic Attack

Jake caught up with Clarice in the emergency room but felt he needed comfort too. Jake couldn't accept the fact his baby girl might be pregnant.

"Why?" he thought.

After Clarice had an EKG or electrocardiogram, the doctors advised her that she suffered a panic attack, which can imitate a heart attack. Both Jake and Clarice were relieved. They needed to get back to their little girl who was going to need them more now. They were approaching Brittany's room when the doctor pulled them aside. The doctor advised them that he had performed a urine HCG or human chorionic gonadotropin test to determine pregnancy hormone levels in Brittany's blood. The doctor regretfully informed the parents of the devastating news.

"Well, I am so sorry to inform you that Brittany's nightmare continues. She is very pregnant. The dates do in fact, coincide with the levels of HCG found in Brittany's blood."

Clarice, sobbing, advised the doctor not to tell Brittany anything. "I will tell her. Please, let it be me that breaks the news to her. I beg you!"

The doctor respected her wishes and didn't tell Brittany about her pregnancy.

"It wasn't fair. Why? Why Brittany? She was smart and beautiful. How can someone change another person's life just like that?"

Clarice was trying to fabricate the right way to tell her daughter that after getting raped, tortured, and disfigured she was carrying the child of her rapist. There was no easy way to say it. She couldn't bring herself to do it. She asked Jake if he could do it for her. Jake, however, couldn't bear the thought of breaking such news. He didn't know how she would react to this unwanted pregnancy.

To Jake, Brittany was still his baby girl. No, he was not going to break her heart like that. He couldn't.

She hadn't started rehab for her current injuries; she was still weak. Her parents feared that Brittany would surely fall into major depression because Brittany had had several episodes where she didn't want to eat or speak; she wanted to sleep all day because waking up would force her to have to look at herself and her facial scars were getting the best of her. The pregnancy would eradicate whatever hope she was holding on to.

CHAPTER 18

What's Right and What's Wrong?

Clarice stood still without saying a word to her daughter for a short while. Clarice stood up, tried to ignore the knot she felt in her throat, looked straight into Brittany's eyes, but couldn't give those awful news. She kept the news from her. Two weeks passed, and Clarice still couldn't bring herself to inform her daughter about her pregnancy.

Days past, Brittany still wasn't holding food down and couldn't tolerate the smell of food, perfumes, or medicines. She was throwing up so much so that doctors had to keep her on continuous intravenous infusions, or IV's to keep her hydrated.

Brittany kept asking the doctor, "What is wrong with me? I can't stand this yucky feeling in my stomach and vomiting anymore. Something has to be wrong with me. Please find out what it is!"

The doctor looked at both parents and asked them to join him outside. Once outside, the doctor advised Jake and Clarice to inform Brittany right away about her pregnancy. If not, he was obligated to tell his patient. Jake and Clarice agreed to tell their daughter and begged the doctor not to tell her yet. They begged the doctor for one more day.

The next day, Jake and Clarice walked into Brittany's room. She was finally sleeping. She had been throwing up all morning. Both parents were distressed about Brittany's situation and how her whole life changed instantly. They knew once she woke up and told she was pregnant, her life would not only belong to her. She would have to share the rest of her life with someone whom she would probably despise—the baby she was carrying.

"Brittany dear," her mother called as she pulled on her gown. Brittany didn't answer. "Brittany, honey, Mommy and Daddy have to speak with you. Brittany!"

Brittany, half asleep from the medications, whispered, "What? What's going on? I am sleepy. Let me sleep."

Clarice mumbled, "Brittany, please wake up. We need to talk. It's important we speak now!"

Jake assertively replied, "Brittany, listen to your mother. Wake up!"

Brittany, trying to wake up, whispered, "Okay, I am up already. What is so important that you have to wake me up, this minute?"

Both parents adjusted Brittany's bed and sat her up.

Clarice said, "Brittany, there is no easy way to tell you that you are with child. You are pregnant, sweetie. We are so sorry that we didn't tell you sooner! That is why you keep throwing up. Sorry. We didn't know how to tell you."

Brittany started to cry hysterically. She faced her dad and asked him, "Dad, is it true? Am I pregnant?"

Jake, crying, said, "Yes, sweetie, it's unfortunately true. You are about three months, but we couldn't believe it ourselves. You have to know now before it's too late. You must make a decision about this child you are carrying. You have to decide between getting an abortion and keeping the baby."

Brittany stopped crying and gave both her parents a confused look and questioned, "I thought it was against our religion having an abortion, or is it ignored in this type of situations like mine? If that is the case, I don't understand. Do I have a choice?"

Jake and Clarice stood in shock, speechless. Was their daughter's situation, one that could or should be ignored, and proceed with the abortion?

Clarice answered, "Well, we didn't even think about that, honey. We assumed since it was from that horrible day, you wouldn't want to keep it."

Brittany said, "Dad, what do you think I should do?"

Jake replied, "Well, I didn't want to pressure you in any way, so I didn't think you would want it either."

Were they wrong to think that this life inside Brittany meant nothing, was nothing, and should be aborted? They didn't have the answers, but they promised her they would find out.

In the meantime, Brittany was left to dwell on, what, if anything, she should do with what life had thrown her.

ABOUT THE AUTHOR

Nati Carrillo was born in Edcouch, Texas, and is a resident of Weslaco. She is a graduate of the University of Texas at Brownsville with a master's degree in nursing. She is a board-certified nurse practitioner. She is the author of one of two books: *Bullies Create Bullies*, a fiction/biography that speaks to preteens and teenagers who so commonly face bullies in their daily lives and encourages her readers to speak up because bullying does not have to be part of their normal life, and bullies are not always big and ugly. *The Slippery Slopes of Consequences* is, a fiction story of irony, of how one simple mistake leads to an even more complicated chain of events for the entire Wee family and that mistakes, no matter how small, affect the entire family.

CPSIA information can be obtained
at www.ICGtesting.com
Printed in the USA
LVHW031432050219
606471LV00001B/65/P